CELEBRATING THE CITY OF BRUSSELS

Celebrating the City of Brussels

Walter the Educator

Silent King Books

SILENT KING BOOKS

SKB

Copyright © 2024 by Walter the Educator

All rights reserved. No part of this book may be reproduced in any manner whatsoever without written permission except in the case of brief quotations embodied in critical articles and reviews.

First Printing, 2024

Disclaimer
This book is a literary work; the story is not about specific persons, locations, situations, and/or circumstances unless mentioned in a historical context. Any resemblance to real persons, locations, situations, and/or circumstances is coincidental. This book is for entertainment and informational purposes only. The author and publisher offer this information without warranties expressed or implied. No matter the grounds, neither the author nor the publisher will be accountable for any losses, injuries, or other damages caused by the reader's use of this book. The use of this book acknowledges an understanding and acceptance of this disclaimer.

Celebrating the City of Brussels is a little collectible souvenir book that belongs to the Celebrating Cities Book Series by Walter the Educator. Collect them all and more books at WaltertheEducator.com

USE THE EXTRA SPACE TO TAKE NOTES AND DOCUMENT YOUR MEMORIES

BRUSSELS

In the heart of Europe, where cultures blend and twist,

Celebrating the City of Brussels

Brussels stands resplendent, bathed in morning mist.

A city woven from the threads of history's grand design,

Where past and present dance in an eternal intertwine.

Cobblestone streets whisper secrets of yesteryears,

Gothic spires reach skyward, quelling ancient fears.

The Grand Place unfolds like a story yet untold,

With guildhalls glistening in a façade of gold.

Celebrating the City of
Brussels

Manneken Pis, the mischievous child, stands bold and free,

A symbol of the city's humor, of its liberty.

In every corner, chocolate shops allure with sweet delight,

A taste of paradise in every delicate bite.

The Atomium, a futuristic relic, gleams in the sun,

A monument to dreams, to visions yet begun.

Its spheres connect like thoughts in a curious mind,

Exploring realms of science, leaving limits behind.

Parc du Cinquantenaire, with arches grand and green,

Celebrating the City of Brussels

A testament to triumphs, to glories once seen.

Here, the whispers of the leaves sing tales of old,

Of heroes and of battles, of stories brave and bold.

In the cafés, life's a symphony of languages diverse,

French and Dutch in harmony, a beautiful converse.

Over a steaming cup of coffee, dreams are shared,

In Brussels, every soul finds a place that's fair.

Art is life in every mural, every stroke and shade,

From Magritte's surreal worlds to Rubens' grand parade.

Museums stand like guardians of the culture's core,

Preserving every fragment, every lore.

Through each season, Brussels dons a different hue,

In spring, the blooms of tulips; in winter, the frosty dew.

Autumn paints the city in hues of amber and gold,

While summer's warmth enlivens, breaking every cold.

Markets bustle with a vibrant, rhythmic beat,

From seafood at Sainte-Catherine to antiques on the street.

Waffles sizzle, luring with their honeyed scent,

Each bite a memory, a moment well spent.

The river Senne, though hidden now from sight,

Once cradled the city, its lifeblood and light.

Now, beneath the surface, it flows silent and deep,

Celebrating the City of Brussels

A reminder of the city's layers, secrets it keeps.

Brussels, a mosaic, so vast,

Of nations, and of peoples, a bridge to future, past.

Each district tells a story, each alley hums a tune,

From Anderlecht's traditions to Ixelles' afternoon.

Celebrating the City of Brussels

ABOUT THE CREATOR

Walter the Educator is one of the pseudonyms for Walter Anderson. Formally educated in Chemistry, Business, and Education, he is an educator, an author, a diverse entrepreneur, and he is the son of a disabled war veteran. "Walter the Educator" shares his time between educating and creating. He holds interests and owns several creative projects that entertain, enlighten, enhance, and educate, hoping to inspire and motivate you. Follow, find new works, and stay up to date with
Walter the Educator™ at
WaltertheEducator.com.

www.ingramcontent.com/pod-product-compliance
Lightning Source LLC
LaVergne TN
LVHW012048070526
838201LV00082B/3856